Crombie Jardine
PUBLISHING LIMITED

Unit 17, 196 Rose Street, Edinburgh EH2 4AT
www.crombiejardine.com

This edition was first published by
Crombie Jardine Publishing Limited in 2006

ISBN 1-905102-73-9

Written by Stuart Macfarlane
Illustrations by Rob Smith and Helen West
Designed by www.glensaville.com
Printed & bound in the United Kingdom by
William Clowes Ltd, Beccles, Suffolk

CONTENTS

INTRODUCTION

Neds... loathe them or not, sadly it's no longer politically correct to ship them all off to desolate antipodean islands. So, while we are stuck with them, it makes sense to at least try to understand them. The first step in doing this is to gain an insight into their language for only then can we get into the hearts and minds of this subclass that terrorises our streets.

This little dictionary provides a window into the underworld of NedVille. Not only will it allow you to translate what Neds are saying, it will give you an appreciation of their culture and values.

By understanding their background, beliefs, and lack of ambition, you may even begin to feel an affinity with Neds. And who knows, soon you may be dressing up in white trackies and Burberry cap and greeting your friends with a cordial, "Ay ya muppet, gonnae pass ra Buckie." Well perhaps this is taking things a little bit too far. Instead, why not just enjoy the book and have a good laugh at the Neds' expense – after all, from cradle to grave, the lazy little bastards are living at your expense.

NED FACT FILE

* The average Ned wears 6.2lbs of bling – the total value of all this jewellery is a staggering £9.74.

7

* The average age when a Nedette becomes a mother is thirteen. By bizarre coincidence this is also the IQ of the average Nedette.

* For every three Neds that are locked up in prison another four are born.

* The average Ned eats 643 burgers and drinks 1,203 cans of Irn Bru each year.

* The average age when a Ned is first sent to prison is 13¾. Nedettes, on the other hand,

8

receive their first stint inside at the age of 13¼: clear proof that Nedettes mature much earlier than their male counterparts.

* Should a Ned survive to the age of 80, he will have spawned nine Childneds, eighty-one grand-Childneds, seven hundred and twenty-nine great-grand-Childneds and six thousand five hundred and sixty-one great-great-grand-Childneds. This is scary!

* If Neds were dropped from the top of Edinburgh Castle at

the rate of one every fifteen seconds, it would make an awful lot of people happy.

10

BASIC TRANSLATIONS

can't	=	cannae
couldn't	=	couldnae
didn't	=	didnae
do	=	dae
down	=	doon
from	=	frae
gave	=	gied
girlfriend	=	burd
home	=	hame
i	=	ah
i am	=	ah'm
i have	=	ah've
into	=	intae
my	=	ma
myself	=	masel'

no	=	nae
not	=	no'
on	=	oan
our	=	oor
the	=	ra
to	=	tae
was not	=	wisnae
will you	=	gonna
with	=	wi'
yes	=	aye
you	=	ya
you're	=	ur
your	=	yer

RA NED
PATTER, A-Z

A

AMBITION

passive noun

The burning desire in the heart of every Ned to reach pension age without doing a day's work. In the good old days any self-respecting hard-man would 'do a bank job'. But in today's namby-pamby world, the average Ned is barely motivated enough to get off his arse and relieve an old age pensioner of her shopping money.

ASBO

noun

The **A**nti **S**ocial **B**ehaviour **O**rder marks a Nedling's passage into full Nedhood. This coming-of-age usually occurs between the age of four and seven and is a great cause for celebration in NedVille society.

B

BAMPOT

vulgar noun

The term 'bampot' has for some time been used to mean 'a crazy person'. In Ned speak, however, it's often used almost affectionately when addressing a friend – as in "Ur fur a doing fur nicking ma burd ya wee fuckin' bampot."

BAMSTICK

refined vulgar noun

Similar term to bampot but used by the more cultured Ned, for example, "Yon Van Gough wis a fuckin' bamstick – his pictures o' matchstick men are pure shite."

BANJOED

discordant verb

Should you meet a Ned in the high street who asks if you would

17

like to be 'banjoed', do not be fooled into thinking he wishes to serenade you with a musical instrument. The phrase is merely a courtesy warning that you will be shortly be rushing to A&E.

BANK JOB

noun

Neds dream of becoming as infamous as Ronnie Briggs by doing a daring bank job. They imagine themselves living a life of luxury filled with masses of bling, all the burgers they could ever eat, quality skunk, buckets of Buckie, and a different burd for every day of the week. Pure fantasy – there's as much chance of a Ned robbing a bank as there is of him opening an account in one.

BAR-L

cushy noun

A holiday camp for Neds. Similar to Butlins but without the need to slop out. Loved so much by Neds that they return annually to get a break from the wife and weans.

BARRAS

noun

Nestling in the east end of Glasgow, this Nedish market is *the* place to buy (or steal) everything from counterfeit Adidas to counterfeit Zoo York. It's also the first place to go to buy back your possessions after your house has been burgled.

BASTARD

noun

A Nedling born out of wedlock.

adulterated adjective

A disagreeable person – and as Neds find everyone disagreeable they even call their best friends 'bastards'.

It is rather an ironic term as indeed most Neds are bastards – in both uses of the word.

BATH

noun

A utility used by Neds for washing their Pit Bull terriers.

BAWBAG

noun

a. Ned term for a scrotum.
b. Derogatory name for an annoying or stupid person.

Typical usage: "Aaaaagghhhh – you kicked me in ra bawbag ya big fuckin' bawbag!"

BEAD RATTLER

devout noun

Religious hatred is very much a part of Ned culture. Out of this come many phrases to describe people of the 'wrong' religion. Bead Rattler is one of the politer terms and conjures up a picture of a devoted supporter sitting at Celtic Park fingering his rosary while praying for a goal.

BEAZER

adjective

An expression meaning 'gosh, that was rather a pleasurable and unexpected event to have occurred' used by Neds when something really good happens. For example, should a Ned find a wallet lying on the street he would say, "Oh ya beazer – now Ah can get totally rat-arsed fur a week."

BINGO BUS

noun

An affectionate term for a police van. So named because when your number's called, you end up getting slung into the back of one.

BITCH

noun

The Ned term for someone of the 'female' gender. Bitch can be used as both a derogatory term and a complimentary term. Typical examples:

"She's a bitch." ("That wee minger won't have sex with me.")
"That's my bitch." ("That's the minger I'm currently shagging.")

BLING

noun

Bling is massive jewellery intended to display decadence and wealth. Generally stolen from Argos or Woolworths or found in 'Lucky Bags'. Bling has its own hallmarking system:

Mark 101: indicates that it's 2ct gold.

Mark 999: indicates that it's made from gold recycled from stolen goods.

Mark 覊然下: indicates that the item is genuine Chinese crap.

BLOOTERED

adjective

A trance-like state induced by consuming vast quantities of Lanliq, Buckfast, cheap house white, turpentine, and, on festive occasions such as funerals, Carlsberg Special. Neds enter this state at around the age of seven and remain in it constantly until they are laid to rest at the age of thirty-seven.

BOGGIN

adjective

A Ned term for something that is smelly or foul tasting. So, for example, when a Ned eats a Chicken Tikka Masala that's been lying under the sofa for three days he might be heard to say, "This chow is pure boggin, man!"

BOTTLE MERCHANT

noun

Not to be confused with a purveyor of fine wine (which is of course a 'vino vendor'). In Ned speak a bottle merchant is a coward – for example any person who, while being chibbed or mugged, is too old or infirm to fight back.

BOOZER

noun

Used instead of the English term, 'public house'. A Ned will happily get pissed at any boozer that he's not currently banned from.

BOUNCER

hard noun

A bouncer is a thug employed to stand at the entrance of a pub or club and beat up people as they try to enter. In NedVille the bouncer will carefully frisk Neds and Nedettes for weapons. Anyone found not carrying one will be given a suitable knife or broken bottle.

BUCKET

noun

A bucket is a cylindrical vessel used for catching, holding, and carrying liquids or solids. However, the ever-ingenious Ned scum have discovered that it's a convenient container for smoking hash. For the more refined Ned it's also a handy alternative to the duvet when puking up a three-day-old Chicken Tikka Masala.

BUCKFAST (BUCKIE)

noun

An abridged version of 'Buckfast Tonic Wine'. This is a fortified beverage made by the Benedictine monks at Buckfast Abbey in Devon, England. Ironically, what began as a medicinal drink for the wealthy has ended up being used by scum to get blootered on the cheap! Oh well – perhaps the Holy Spirit is in this lowly spirit and that will be the saving grace of Neds!

BUCKFAST COMMANDO

injudicious noun

The gladiator of modern civilization who's intoxicated bravado enthuses him with the courage to walk the full length of Sauchiehall Street in a straight (straightish) line without giving way to pensioners, waste bins, Big Issue marketing executives, vomit piles and fast moving cars.

BUFTY

noun

Used by Neds instead of the English 'homosexual'. Due to the similarity to the term 'buftie' which is a mutated version of 'birthday', many a Ned has had a doing for asking a friend, "Do ya want tae cum tae ma buftie party?"

BUNTY

noun

A bunty is anyone who's the subject of the Neds' favourite

hobby – thugery. So who makes a good bunty? You do! A Ned high on nail varnish doesn't give a toss whether you're a nine-year-old blind girl or a ninety-year-old cripple – he'll happily give anyone a doing.

BURD

common noun

'Burd' or 'ra burd', as she is more often referred to, is a Ned's steady girlfriend. The reciprocal term used by a Nedette for her current boyfriend is 'that fuckin' waster'.

BUS SHELTER

accommodating noun

A bus shelter is to a Ned what a cave was to prehistoric man. It is his refuge from the cruel world, his boudoir for procreation, a place to create primitive art with a spray can and, of course, a fine place to set on fire unceremoniously after drinking a bucket of Buckie.

C

CANNIE

auxiliary verb

Used in the phrase 'ah cannie' which translates literally as 'I am too bloody lazy to'. This is one of the Neds' favourite expressions. Typical examples of usage are:

"Ah cannie get oot of bed."
"Ah cannie get a job."
"Ah cannie dae ma homework, pass ma exams, then go tae university so Ah can become

a useful member o' society."

CAR

felonious noun

Non-Ned Car: A vehicle of average value £10,000 that contains a stereo worth £100.

Ned Car: An unroadworthy heap of rust worth less than £100 but containing £10,000 worth of stereo and accessories.

CARGO

noun

Neds buy all their shopping from the off-sales and 'cargo' is their word for a 'carry out' or 'Judas Iscariot'. A typical week's cargo is 40 bags of crisps, 200 fags, 60 cans of lager and 10 bottles of Buckie. If money is really tight a Ned can survive without the crisps.

CHAV

noble noun

A Chav is a hooligan who inhabits the slum areas of Edinburgh. Believing that they are far superior to their Glaswegian neighbours, the Edinburgh folk prefer to give their Neds this much posher name.

CHEERS

transitive verb

Never wishing to use the self-abasing term 'thanks', a Ned

will say 'cheers' instead. Cheers is always followed by 'man' as in, "That wis a dead good shag – cheers, man." The wide usage of the expression 'cheers, man' is the reason most Nedettes have a sexual identity problem.

CHESS

cerebral noun

An intellectual activity enjoyed by Neds over a few dozen bottles of Buckie. "Ah take yer pawn en-passant ya cunt and it's forced mate in six – innit," is an oft heard Ned expression – NOT!

CHIB

noun

Taken from the Latin 'chibaninnocentbystander', this is a Ned term for an easily concealable weapon such as a flick knife, pickaxe, or Heckler Koch MP-5 submachine gun.

CHIPPIE

noun

Ned speak for 'fish and chip shop'. The chippie is as close to home cooking as a Ned ever gets. It provides that vitamin-enriched delicacy, the fried mars bar, which helps give the Ned his characteristic spotty-little-fucker complexion.

CHRISTMAS

noun

Neds love Christmas – it gives them the opportunity to show off their style and status. Come 1st November, every Ned's house will be tastefully decorated with enough flashing lights to bring down the National Grid. Of course, thanks to a bit of amateur rewiring, Neds never have to pay expensive electricity bills.

CHURCH

noun

All Neds visit church once in their lives – horizontally in fake Burberry coffins!

CLAIMED

transitive verb

In olden days when a man was insulted he threw down the gauntlet to challenge the wrongdoer to a dual with pistols. Keeping up the romantic chivalry of old, if a Ned is dishonoured, for example by someone crossing his path, he will proclaim, "Ur claimed". Having given ample warning of his intent, he will then thrust a blade into the scoundrel's stomach.

COMPLIMENT

exceptional noun

There are only one thousand and two hundred words in the Ned's limited vocabulary. Five hundred and forty of these are derogatory terms such as bawbag, muppet, and slag.

Around three hundred words are used to describe drink and drugs. Over two hundred words are available when discussing theft, mugging and assault. There are even twelve words to describe the length of a Nedette's mini skirt. However, when it comes to giving someone a compliment, Neds have absolutely no words at their disposal.

CONTRACEPTION

fucking noun

If a Ned manages to jammie open the pub's Durex machine, he may use a condom during sex. His prime reason for doing so is not to avoid putting the Nedette in 'the family way' – but rather to avoid having to make yet another trip to the VD clinic.

COUSIN

intimate noun

In NedVille, due to a combination of inferior housing, unsocial drinking, and drug abuse, inbreeding is prevalent. A Ned may thus confidently use the term cousin for anyone who lives within two miles of his house.

COUPON

noun

Used in place of the English word 'face'. The Nedette's coupon will always be covered in an inch of foundation and blusher to make it look less vile. The Ned, on the other hand, takes pride in having a coupon that shows off his bravery and will proudly display his numerous scars, slashes, and other 'war wounds'.

CUNT

vulgar noun

A slang expression for the English word 'vagina'. Of course, when a Ned yells at someone, "You're a fuckin' cunt!", he doesn't mean you're a fuckin' vagina – what he's really saying is you're a fuckin' dobber [see p.55].

D

DEALER

felon noun

Someone who provides a social service in NedVille. The local drug dealer is often the only person who cares about the welfare of a young Ned. A dealer can be heard making encouraging comments to his young charges such as, "See you, ya wee crackhead – if you don't pay for the stuff tomorrow Ah'm gonna fuckin' kill you."

DECIBEL

noun

A measurement of the Nova's Magablaster sound system's ability to cause acute deafness. Anything under an earth-quaking 1000 dB is considered only suitable for wimps and Sassenachs.

DETOX

transitive verb

Detox is when a Ned completely abstains from glue, drugs,

cigarettes, and alcohol. The main reason that a Ned enters a period of detox is that he's sleeping. These sessions have been known to last as long as six hours.

DOBBER

diminutive noun

Used in place of 'penis' in Ned speak. A Ned never calls his penis (or indeed any penis) a dobber but he does call all his friends dobbers – implying that they are all penises. So, in effect, he takes pleasure in hanging about with penises – which tends to suggest he's a bit of a prick himself!

DOING

excruciating noun

A doing is something that is given. Neds tend to give them to random people in the street who are younger, smaller and weaker than them. The consequences of receiving a doing are likely to be: a black eye, slashed face, bleeding nose, and broken limbs. Doings are best avoided!

DRUM (THE)

popper noun

An abridged version of Drumchapel – a large NedVille suburb of Glasgow adjacent to the posh area of Bearsden. Drive through The Drum and you will not see a single Ned – they are all in Bearsden wasting the cars, burgling houses, and trying to tempt the Poshettes into going back to the slums for a quick shag.

DSS

benefactorial noun

The **D**ole for **S**croungers and **S**windlers is the main source of income for Nedkind. Each week every Ned and Nedette receives: Family Support, Unemployment Benefit, Disability Benefit, Multiple Addiction Supplementary Benefit, Bereavement Benefit, Cold Weather Payments, Crisis Loans, Incapacity Benefit, Industrial Injuries Disablement Benefit, Jobseeker's Allowance, Maternity Allowance and numerous other payments. Pick pocketing, mugging, drug dealing, protection rackets, and the entrepreneurial use of a crowbar supplement this meagre income.

DUG

canoun

Refers to the English term 'dog'. The dug is the ultimate fashion accessory for the Ned who aims to impress. A rottweiler straining at the leash, growling through flesh-ripping teeth, helps give its owner that coveted hard-man look.

DUNTED

intransitive verb

To be dunted is to be a little bit drunk. But, to be honest, saying that a Ned is a little bit drunk is as ridiculous as saying that the deceased was stabbed a little bit through the heart.

E

EDUCATION

abstract noun

Neds are not excluded from the education system – in fact, very often both mother and daughter are studying for their GCSE in Scrounging at the same time. This is handy, for it enables the truant officer to kill two birds with the one stone (metaphorically speaking).

ELECTRIC SOUP

noun

Any kind of cheap, strong booze is referred to as electric soup. Shocking!

EMDY

noun

A contraction of the English term 'anybody'. The word is invariably used in conjunction with the word 'gorra' to produce the questioning phrase 'Emdy gorra'. This is then suffixed with a variety of works such as 'fag', 'joint' or 'fuckin' clue where Ah live'.

EMPLOYMENT

superfluous noun

Not all Neds are complete wasters: some manage to hold down a job for weeks at a time. Our research shows that the most suitable jobs for Neds are as follows:

Junior lavvie attendant; crash test dummy; onion peeler for McDonald's; guinea pig at a medical research centre.

ERRA

exclamation

A mutilated version of the English expression, 'Oh my gosh, there is the'. It is common to hear a Ned's distressing cries of, "Erra Polis!", or when high on glue, "Erra purple elephant salsa dancing on ra ceiling!"

EXPLOITATION

noun

When marketing men put together a range of trashy bling by Nedette idol Jordan and sell it through their favourite shop, Argos, this is called exploitation. These colourful glass sparklers in the shape of bras and panties are pure must-have accessories for every gullible little Nedette.

F

FANNY-STRUCK

mythological noun

When a Ned says that he's 'fanny-struck' he means that he's 'in love'. In actual fact, he met a wee minger at the club but was so pissed he mistook her for a Kylie Minogue look-alike and wrote his phone number across her stomach with lipstick. On the follow-up date, if he's sober he will run a mile, if drunk another Nedling will enter the world.

FAST FOOD

noxious noun

Neds exist on cheap foods that require the minimum amount of preparation – crisps, chocolate and chewing gum are favourites. If celebrating a special occasion, such as the bursting of a pluke or the birth of a seventh Nedling, a trip to the chippy or McDonald's would be in order.

FAILURE

common noun

Neds do not know the meaning of 'failure' – and 517,042 other words.

FOOTBALL

noun

Celtic! Rangers! Hearts! Clydebank! Caledonian Thistle!! The noble game is the cornerstone of Ned culture. While the players battle it out on the pitch, the Neds have their own battle to get on with. And any defenceless supporter who falls foul of the

Neds' attack will just have to pay the penalty.

FOREPLAY

lustful noun

The intimate act of seduction as carried out by a Ned. This involves getting a Nedette pissed on cheap cider then carrying her off to his four poster bus shelter for a bit of nookie.

FREEDOM

contradictory noun

Being released from all the comforts and amenities of Barlinnie to live in the squalor of a two-room council flat with a drug-crazed Nedette and her six greetin' Nedlings.

FUCK

illiterate expletive

A universal word used by a Ned to hide his lack of education. Acting as a replacement for conventional words, it allows a Ned to string a full sentence together. E.g. "Aw fucking gonna geeze ra fucker for fuck sake ya fuck-face." Strangely, other Neds can understand these fucking sentences fucking implicitly.

?!

G

GCSE

whimsical noun

A 'pass' at E level in Woodwork, Knitting or Domestic Violence is good enough for wild celebrations in any Ned household. A Ned with two such passes is considered a genius – any with more than two is a considered a bunty [see p.35] and dealt with appropriately.

GLASGOW KISS

noun

A Glasgow Kiss is a greeting that is not exclusive to Glasgow. Indeed, many a Glasgow Kiss has been given in Greenock, Glenrothes and even Geilenkirchen (though Geilenkirchen Kiss doesn't have the same ring to it). A Glasgow Kiss is given by striking the forehead against the beneficiary's head. Targeting the nose provides the most pleasing effect.

GLUE

tacky noun

A strong liquid adhesive obtained by boiling animal parts such as bones, hides, and hooves. Neds use it for building model aeroplanes, mending broken vases and sniffing from a poly bag until rat-arsed and mindless.

GONEREA

distributive noun

Something that a Nedette gives freely but cannot spell.

74

GRASS

distractive noun

One of the many Ned terms for 'Marijuana'. It is harvested from the flowering portion and leaves of the hemp plant and contains over 400 chemicals including Tetrahydrocannabinol. But Neds don't want to know that! All they want to know is that, when smoked from a bong or joint, it produces hallucinogenic effects that allow a temporary escape from the hell of NedVille.

GUY FAUX NIGHT

noun

A night when Neds get completely bevied, fall into the bonfire and get 3rd-degree burns (the only degree a Ned ever achieves). Other celebrations on this special occasion include setting fire to bus shelters, putting rockets through letter boxes, and stuffing bangers up cats' arses.

76

77

H

HAIRY

noun

A 'Hairy' is a girl who dresses like a slut, loves to binge drink, wears masses of bling, and is willing to shag anything with a dick. By definition all Nedettes are Hairies.

HAUTE CUISINE

entrée noun

Are you bloody joking?!?!

HAUTE COUTURE

cult noun

Neds and Nedettes have unique tribal uniforms that make them stand out from the crowd.

Ned-Style: Burberry baseball cap worn at a jaunty angle. White tracksuit by Kappa – with the bottoms tucked into socks. White trainers or Timberland boots. If going 'shopping' at the mall, a zip-up hoodie will also be worn. All this is set off with as much bling as the Ned has managed to nick.

Nedette-Style: Orange tan courtesy of Tan-a-Reef. An ultra short mini skirt. Huge earrings. Faux-leather jacket from H&M. A skin-tight t-shirt that stops three inches above a gold-plated navel stud. All set off with a dash of bad attitude.

HEE HAW

noun

Ned speak for the English expression 'bugger all'. Often used as part of the courting ritual between Ned and Nedette. The Ned will inquire, "Fancy a shag?" The Nedette will reply indignantly, "Ur gettin' hee haw!" Fifteen minutes later they're going at it like dogs in heat at the nearest bus shelter.

HER MAJESTY'S PLEASURE

noun

Most Neds are at some stage detained 'at Her Majesty's pleasure' – usually in solitary at a high-security prison. Upon release, they explain their absence rather more romantically by saying, "Ah'm a spy wae ra MI5 but dinnae tell emdy".

HOME COOKING

passive verb

Spurred on by the likes of Jamie Oliver and Gordon Ramsey, more and more Neds are taking to home cooking. For the really adventurous this entails stuffing a stir fry in the microwave for twenty seconds while opening six bottles of Lanliq.

HOODIE

obscure noun

A hoodie is a sweatshirt with a hood and is an invaluable garment for a Ned. Not only does it hide his identity from prying CCTV cameras but also during sex it offers him anonymity and thus protection from expensive paternity suits.

I

IBEEFA

hedonistic noun

A Spanish holiday resort on the Nediterranean. Neds go there by the thousands on their annual pilgrimage to Clubland. Twelve Neds can squeeze into an apartment that costs less than ten bottles of Buckie to rent – so there's plenty of dole money left for getting totally blootered.

INNIT

assertive expression

An appendage to any and every sentence muttered by a Ned in his attempt to obtain cordial agreement from his peers – as in, "Yer Nova's a heap o' fuckin' shite – innit?"

IQ

lingering verb

What a Ned does outside the Post Office on a Monday in order to obtain money for smack, Irn Bru and crisps.

IRN BRU (BARRBRU)

cordial noun

Irn Bru is a mild citrus drink that tastes like rusting old girders. Nevertheless, despite competition from Buckfast, Tennents Lager, Carlsburg Special, Bad Jelly, Metz, Black Jack, Grolsch, and countless others, Irn Bru is the Ned's 'other national drink'.

J

JEN UP

fallacious adjective

'Jen up' is the Neds way of saying 'honestly'.

So when the judge asks a Ned, "Do you deny attempting to steal exhibit A?", he will reply, "I wiz only wantin' tae see it in ra daylight. Jen up – I hud nae intention o' stealing ra fuckin' telly."

JOYRIDE

verb

Joyride conjures up pictures of cruising along a quiet coastal road on the way to a pleasurable picnic in the countryside. However, in Ned speak it has a completely different meaning. For Neds, joyriding is stealing a car, driving recklessly, and then writing it off with the aid of a tree.

JUNIOR-JINER'S MATE

inert noun

A very ambitious Ned may eventually achieve the status of tea boy on a building site. This pinnacle of his career seldom lasts long as even brewing a cup of tea is too taxing for a Ned's feeble brain.

JUNK FOOD

noun

To Neds, this is a wide range of inedible foods including lettuce, yogurt, pasta, and banana.

L

LOVE

passive verb

It would be foolish to think that Neds and Nedettes do not fall in love – for indeed they are driven by the same hormones as normal people. However, theirs is not the Romeo and Juliet type of love. Rather it's the type that results in six weans, a messy divorce, and several court restraining orders.

M

MALL

collective noun

A shopping area where every self-respecting Ned has, on at least six occasions, been banned for shop lifting, pick pocketing, causing GBH or, more commonly, simply existing.

MASSIVE

collective noun

In the way that you get a Dread of Tern, a Gang of Elk, a Mutation of Thrushes, a Bevy of Roe Deer, and a Troubling of Goldfish the name for a group of Neds is a Massive.

Other commonly used names are bastards, scum and fuck-wits.

MATALAN

proletariat noun

This exclusive chain of shops is the Harrods of NedVille. When a Nedette is really flush, like after a win at bingo, she will go to Matalan to nick a few pairs of faux designer trackies.

MATE

noun

Refers to the English 'friend' When a Ned uses the phrase 'mate', it is usually preceded by one of the following:

"Got a light", "Geeza fiver" or "Ur fur a doing".

MAW

puerile noun

Used in place of 'mother' in Ned speak. Any Nedette over the age of twelve will be maw to at least one Nedling. Motherhood brings with it huge responsibilities – there's the council house to trash, family allowance to squander, and, in preparation for a long day in front of the telly, dumping of the litter at nursery school.

MAX'D

verb

When a twenty-year-old rust bucket of a Nova has been accessorized with £5,000 worth of neon lights, black tints, mega-power sound system, Mulberry bucket seats, alloys, aero flaps, and go-faster stickers it is said to be max'd.

McDONALD'S

noun

Up to the age of twelve a Ned thinks McDonald's is the only place that hot food comes from. Thereafter he discovers that it's the only place he's likely to get a job.

MENTO

noun

As in stupid; extreme foolishness or behaviour that demonstrates it. Typical usage: "Ya pure mad mento muppet!"

MINCE

noun

When a Ned says that something is 'mince' he means 'nonsense'. It has been suggested that this term comes from 'minced beef' but that is surely ridiculous as no Ned could ever afford such a luxury.

MINGER

noun

The Ned speak equivalent of the English term, 'absolutely stomach-

churningly hideous person'.
This is how a Ned describes
the sexual attractiveness of a
Nedette twenty minutes before
getting pissed and shagging
her senseless.

MINI SKIRT

diminutive noun

There are two main reasons that
Nedettes choose to wear ultra-
short mini skirts:

1) Flimsy little skirts can be stuffed into a handbag making them easy to nick from H&M.

2) Nedettes are all sluts.

MOBILE PHONE

communicative noun

A must-have accessory for all Neds and Nedettes. They even have their own special tariff – Steal As You Go.

M.O.T.

noun

A certificate of a car's roadworthiness bought by Neds at the pub. The advantage of these M.O.T.s is that trivial details, like registration number and expiry date, don't need to be filled in until the document has to be produced at the police station.

MUCKER

noun

Mucker is a term of endearment used between Neds. For once the Neds have got it right – the 1936 Merriam's Collegiate

Dictionary reports: Mucker – *A coarse vulgar person, esp. one capable of offence against courtesy or honour.*

MUPPET

noun

What do Kermit the Frog, Miss Piggy and Neds have in common? They are all muppets. The difference is that Kermit and Miss Piggy have character and charm whereas Neds are just stupid and repulsive.

102

N

NAN

noun

Ordinary people have grandmothers – Neds have nans. The only difference is that a lady becomes a grandmother around the age of fifty whereas a Nedette becomes a nan at twenty-six.

NED

scum noun

There is no such term as 'Ned' in Ned speak for, of course, a Ned would never refer to himself in such a derogatory way. If asked to describe his kin a Ned would reply, "We're pure dead gallus, man – we're la Buckie de la Buckie o' society."

NEDLING

waster noun

A Nedling is any offspring under six years of age who has not yet received an ASBO. Ever since Ned heroine Paris Hilton was named after a posh hotel in the French capital, it has become popular to name Nedlings after their place of conception. Some recent examples are: Vauxhall, Channel-Tunnel, Uppa-Close, Pierre-Brighton and Inra-Cludgie.

NEDUSA

noun

Derived from the legendary Greek Gorgon, Medusa, who could turn anyone who looked upon her loathsome face into stone.

Nedusa describes a Nedette whose face is so ugly it turns her man to drink.

NICK

noun: A short version of Nicholas, Nick is a common name in NedVille.

noun: A slang name for a prison.

verb: To acquire possessions without the inconvenience of a financial transaction.

So one might hear a Nedette explaining the absence of her

son by saying, "Nick nicked some Nikes and he's doin' a stint in the nick."

NUMPTY

Ned speak for the expression 'bloody useless idiot'. It's often used as a good-humoured rebuke when someone has done something stupid. For example, when a footballer misses a sitter, a Ned on the terrace is sure to shout, "Ye couldnae hit a cow's arse wae a shovel, ya big numpty."

P

PAW

absent noun

The Ned word for 'father'. When a Nedette conceives, it is reasonable to assume that at least one member of the opposite sex was present. However, by the time the Nedling arrives, the father's identity has long since been forgotten or paternity suit contested. Young Neds grow up fantasizing that their paw is a mass murderer or mafia hit man who will one day come to take them away from their abject squalor.

PHILOSOPHY

inane noun

Neds maintain a fairly simple philosophy on existence:

"I think I am a fuckwit, therefore I am."

R

RAT-ARSED

noun

As drinking is a favourite pastime, there are many terms for 'being drunk' in Ned speak. Rat-arsed, blootered, charred, stoshus, dunted, steamin, oot yer face, rubber, blazin, stoavin, steamboats, buzzin, ful eh it, bongoed, mad wae it, mutted, are just a few.

RESPECT

irregular verb

A term unknown to Neds.

ROLE MODELS

noun

Nedettes long to become bright and beautiful like their heroine Jordan. From the moment she gets her first bra, a Nedette starts saving her pocket money to get the boob job that will allow her to become a Page Three model.

ROMANCE

noun

Taking a girl for a candlelit dinner then watching a spectacular ballet performance and afterwards walking hand-in-hand along a moonlit beach is not a Ned's idea of how to romance his sweetheart. If she is very lucky, she might be treated to a fish supper and a can of Special before finding her knickers at her feet in some cold and dingy bus shelter.

S

SCHOOL

awol noun

A place that Neds avoid until the age of sixteen when they are no longer legally obliged to attend. At this point school becomes *the* place to hang out in the hope of picking up a girl or two.

SENGA

noun

Senga is fairly often the name given to the fierce Ned matriarch. Rumour has it that 'Senga' started life because people with the traditional Scottish name Agnes wanted to pass it on to offspring in a more palatable and romantic form and so spelled it backwards.

SHITE

noun

A generic term used to describe everything from a Big Mac that has too much onion on it to a Jaguar with impenetrable locks.

SLAG

vulgar pro-noun

A term used by a Ned to describe any Nedette who will sleep with all his mates but refuses to sleep with him (except when she's pissed or is given a fiver) e.g. his sister.

SOBRIETY

noun

Nae fuckin' chance!

SORTED

noun

Ned equivalent of the expression 'everything is tickety-boo'. So, when a Ned's Nova has had its big end repaired or he finally manages to get his CD collection

into alphabetical order, he will
say, "Sorted, man."

SQUALOR

noun

The living conditions that all
Neds manage to achieve without
effort. The typical Ned's bedroom
will have: fifty empty lager cans
strewn across the floor, piles of
old Sun newspapers balanced
on tables and chairs, bundles of
stinking socks and pants that are
attracting flies, occasional pools
of vomit, and, of course, one inch

of dust on everything. Oh, and somewhere amongst it all – two pet ferrets.

SQUAT

noun

Unlike his sisters, a Ned can't simply have a baby then apply for an all-expenses-paid council house. When a Ned gets kicked out of the family home, he needs to find accommodation of his own. This form of housing is called a 'squat'.

T

TATTOO

noun

It's not true that Nedettes are born with tattoos on their backs and studs protruding from their belly buttons. But certainly, by the time she reaches nursery-school age, no self respecting Nedette would be without these symbols of her class. Where the cost of going to a back-street tattoo artist is prohibitive, a home-job is often done with an old hypodermic and a few bottles of coloured ink.

TV LICENCE

noun

There is a simple rule in NedVille: "Nicked tellies don't need a licence."

TWICKING

apocryphal noun

When high on drink and drugs, groups of Neds often play 'twicking'. This is a game of

120

perilous dares to determine who is the most macho. Carving a tattoo on the arm with a rusty knife and stealing a car are two of the most popular dares.

T.W.O.C.

verb

In its normal use, T.W.O.C. means Taking WithOut Consent. Challenge a Ned who's taking something without your consent and he'll tell you that he's just, "Taking What's Ours, Cunt" – and then give you a Glasgow Kiss [see p.73].

TWOCKER

noun

A Twocker is a Ned who takes a car without consent then ends up F.U.C.K.E.D. against a T.R.E.E.

U

UNCLE

collective noun

A term of endearment used by a Ned to describe all the men who are shagging his maw. Typical use is, "Ah hate all ma fuckin' naucing uncles."

W

WEAN

greetin' noun

The ultimate goal of any Nedette over the age of seven is to have her first wean. The first born to a girl in NedVille is considered very special, for a wean is her passport to a rent-free council house. Most maws put their daughters on the housing list at the age of eight – in anticipation of the happy event.

WEDDING

atypical noun

Contrary to popular belief, Neds do occasionally get married. Sometimes a Ned will do so because he has found the Nedette of his glue-induced dreams but more often it is because he has found a sawn-off shotgun pressed against his chest.

Wedding are always held at the 'Redgie Office' followed by a slap-up meal at KFC's then a good bevie at the Working Men's Social.

Y

YA BADSTAR

nuon

A dyslexic Ned of questionable parentage.

YA DANCER

interjection

Exclamation of delight used when something really good happens. (And let's face it – in the life of a Ned this is a very rare occurrence and must be celebrated.)

So you may observe a Ned who has just bought ten instant lottery tickets yelling, "Oh ya dancer I jist wun two quid!".

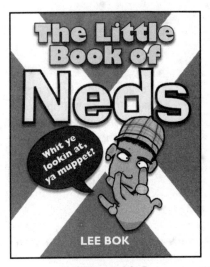

1-905102-30-5
£2.99

127

If you enjoyed this book and
have any comments
or suggestions, please email:
emdy@crombiejardine.com
or visit
www.crombiejardine.com/nedspeak
for Ned jokes.

www.crombiejardine.com